Gaenslen

HORSES!

BY GAIL GIBBONS

HOLIDAY HOUSE / New York

To Olis Thurston

Special thanks to Jodi Kelly and
Daniel J. Kelly, D.V.M. of Stonecliff Animal
Clinic, Bradford, Vermont

Library of Congress Cataloging-in-Publication Data
Gibbons, Gail.
Horses! /by Gail Gibbons.—1st ed.
p. cm.
Summary: Presents information on horses,
including their physical characteristics and behavior.
ISBN 0-8234-1703-4 (hardcover)
ISBN 0-8234-1875-8 (paperback)
1. Horses—Juvenile literature. [1. Horses.] I. Title.
SF302.G53 2003
636.1—dc21
2003041683

In a lush green meadow, a herd of animals is grazing.
One of them neighs. Another shakes its mane. Horses!
What powerful, graceful, and majestic animals they are.

The name EOHIPPUS (EE·o-HIP-us) comes from two Greek words. *EO* means "dawn." *HIPPUS* means "horse."

Horses have been around for a long time. Their earliest ancestors lived about 60 million years ago in what now is known as North America. Scientists named this ancient creature Eohippus. It stood about 15 inches (37.5 cm) tall. Its front feet had four toes and the hind feet had three. Each toe had a small hoof.

DOMESTICATE
also means to TAME.

Over millions of years Eohippus evolved into the horse. The horse migrated to South America, Europe, and Asia before mysteriously disappearing from North America. People first hunted horses for their meat and hide. Then about six thousand years ago people learned they could domesticate horses. They taught them to pull things.

Next, horses were used to carry goods and food. Then people learned to ride them. Eventually warriors on horseback, such as knights, usually could win battles against their enemies that fought on foot.

About five hundred years ago Spanish explorers brought horses back to North America. Over time Native Americans, pioneers, and settlers used more and more horses. Horses plowed fields for crops. They pulled carts, wagons, and carriages. People rode horses and were able to travel faster and further than ever before.

Today there are three basic sizes of horses. The smallest are called ponies. Next are the light horses. The biggest horses are the draft horses. There are many different kinds of purebred horses around the world.

A purebred horse has a mother and father from the same breed. A crossbred horse has at least one parent that is not a purebred.

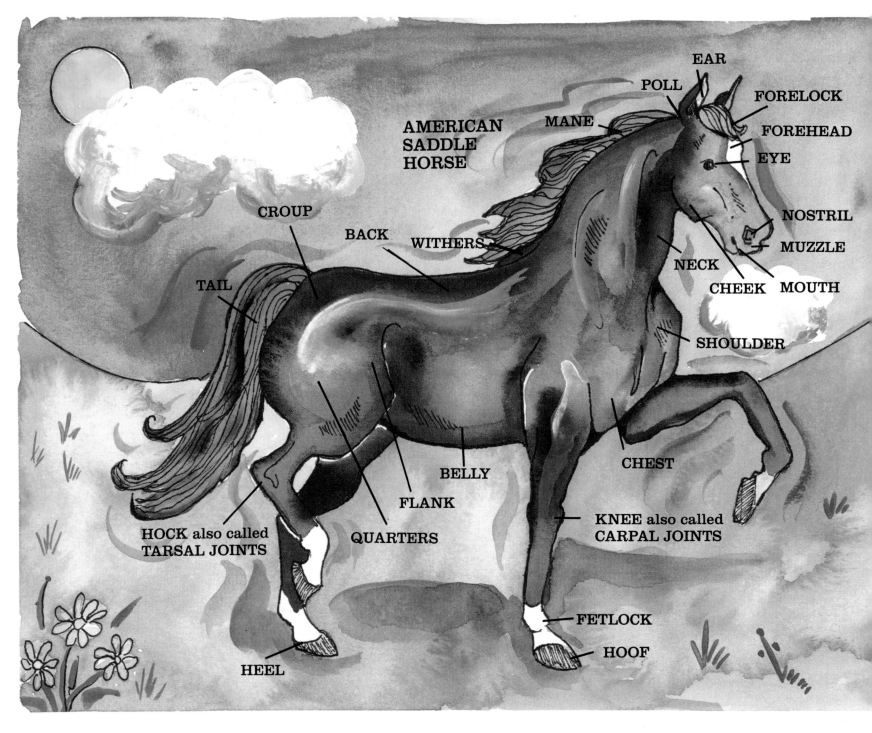

Almost all horses have the same basic characteristics.

WELSH PONY

The WITHERS is the highest point of a horse's shoulder.

HAFLINGER PONY

A horse's height is measured in "hands," from its withers to the ground. One hand equals 4 inches (10 cm). A horse less than 14 hands 2 inches (145 cm) from its withers to the ground is called a pony.

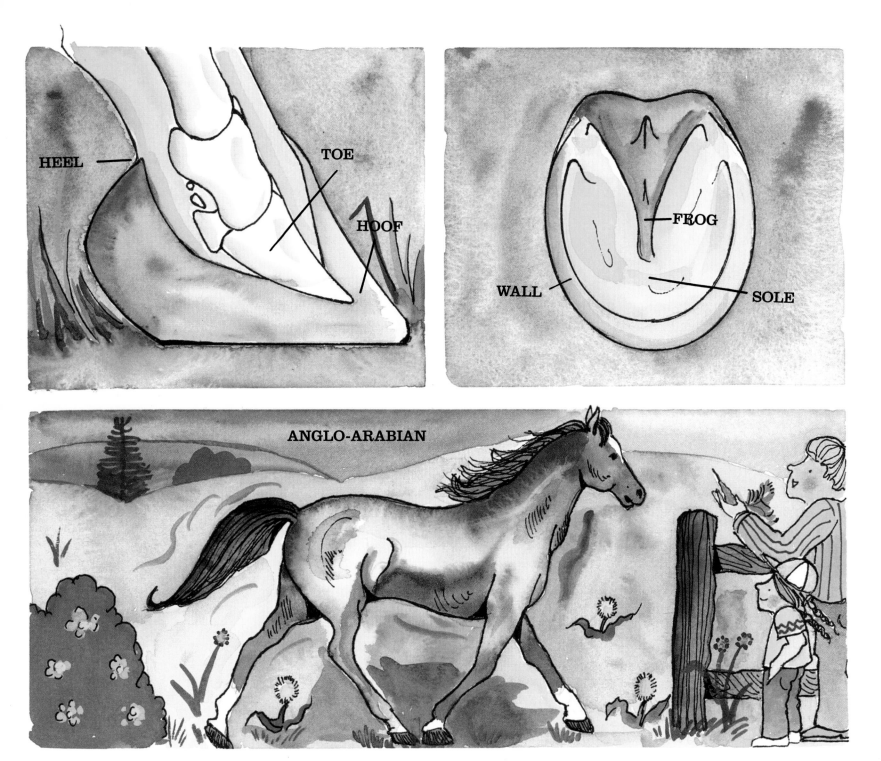

HEEL **TOE** **HOOF** **FROG** **WALL** **SOLE**

ANGLO-ARABIAN

A horse's foot has a heel and a single toe, which fits into a thick toenail called a hoof. The outside layer of a hoof is called the wall. Horses are the only animals that stand on only one toe on each foot.

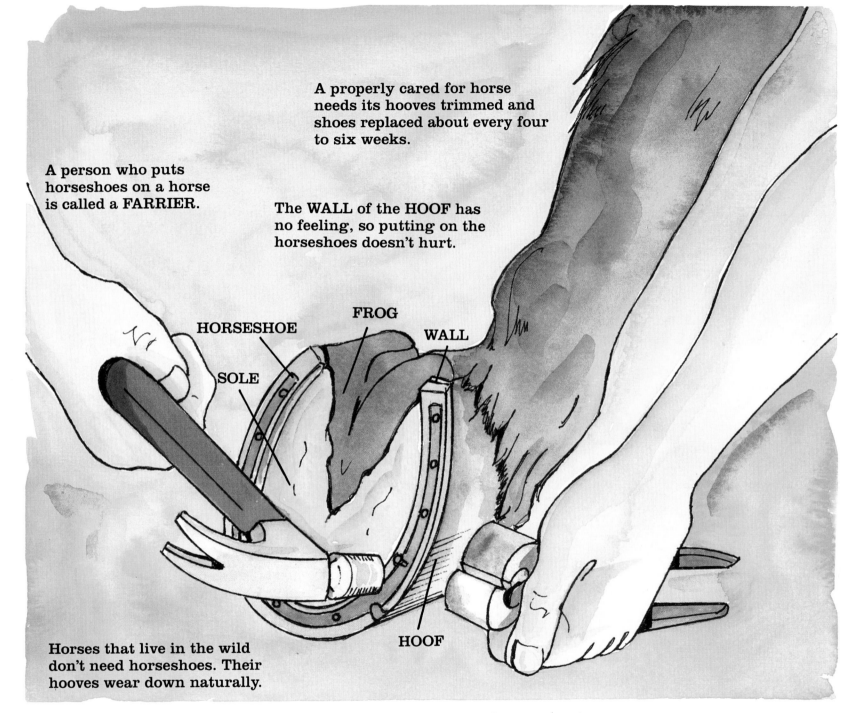

A properly cared for horse needs its hooves trimmed and shoes replaced about every four to six weeks.

A person who puts horseshoes on a horse is called a FARRIER.

The WALL of the HOOF has no feeling, so putting on the horseshoes doesn't hurt.

FROG

HORSESHOE

WALL

SOLE

HOOF

Horses that live in the wild don't need horseshoes. Their hooves wear down naturally.

Horses that are used for riding or for doing work can wear down and damage their hooves. They need to wear horseshoes to protect their hooves. A horseshoe is nailed to the wall of a hoof.

A horse has very strong legs. The two front legs carry most of the horse's body weight when moving. The hind legs provide the thrust forward.

THE GAITS OF A HORSE

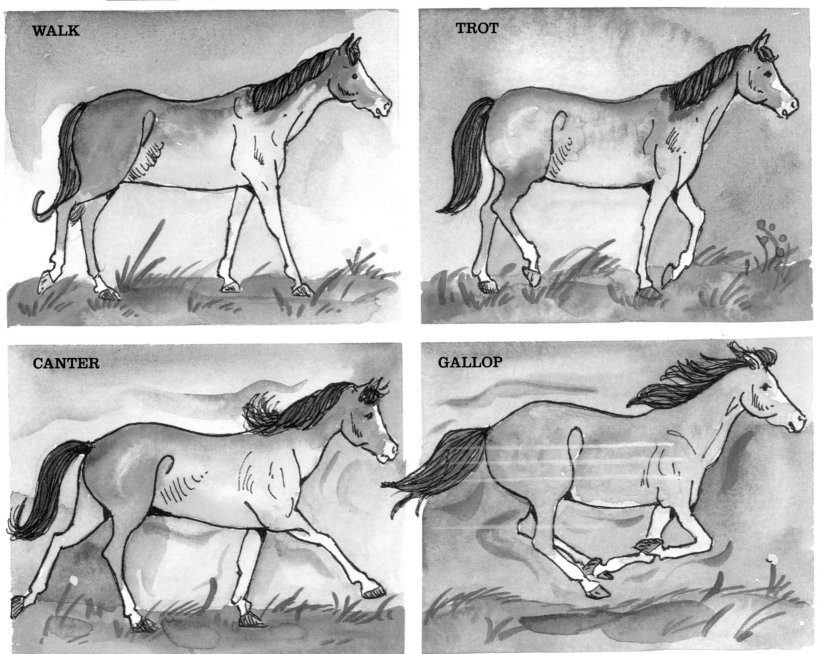

WALK

TROT

CANTER

GALLOP

The way a horse moves its legs and places its hooves on the ground to move forward is called the horse's gait. These gaits go from slow to fast.

A HORSE'S TEETH

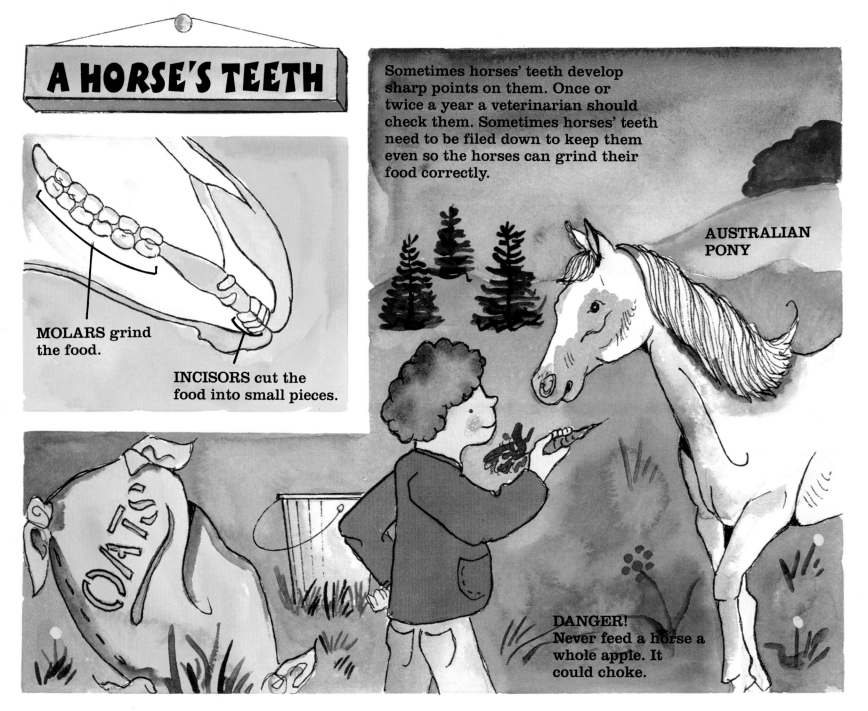

Sometimes horses' teeth develop sharp points on them. Once or twice a year a veterinarian should check them. Sometimes horses' teeth need to be filed down to keep them even so the horses can grind their food correctly.

AUSTRALIAN PONY

MOLARS grind the food.

INCISORS cut the food into small pieces.

OATS

DANGER! Never feed a horse a whole apple. It could choke.

Horses drink a lot of water. They are called herbivores because they don't eat meat. Wild horses and domesticated horses graze on grasses. Domesticated horses are also given oats and other grains for nourishment. Horses enjoy treats such as apple slices, carrots, and sugar cubes.

APPALOOSA

A horse gets all its air for breathing through its nostrils. It doesn't breathe through its mouth as other animals do. It has large, wide nostrils to take large amounts of air into its large lungs. This tremendous breathing power allows a horse to run and run and run.

MUSTANGS

Horses are very social animals. They prefer to live in groups. In the wild a herd of horses is usually made up of a stallion and its mares. One stallion will fight another that is trying to take one of its mares.

Ears that face FORWARD and are UPRIGHT mean the horse is alert.

Ears that are FLAT and POINTING BACK can mean anger or aggression.

When two horses NUZZLE each other, it means friendship.

A short TWITCH of a horse's tail means it is nervous.

REARING means excitement, playfulness, or the show of power.

A horse may BUCK when it is playful or when it tries to get a rider off its back.

Horses can whinny or make other sounds that mean different things. They also communicate using different body movements.

MORGAN

Horses have a better sense of hearing than people do. They also have an excellent sense of smell that can help them recognize each other. Horses are very sensitive to the scent of people.

QUARTER HORSE

Horses have excellent eyesight, which helps protect them in the wild. Their eyes can move independently of each other. That means they can look forward with one eye and behind with the other eye at the same time. The eyes of a horse are larger than the eyes of any other land animal.

A father horse is called a SIRE.

MISSOURI FOX TROTTER

Sometimes a mare gives birth to two foals.

A female foal is called a FILLY.

A mother horse is called a DAM.

MISSOURI FOX TROTTER

A male foal is called a COLT.

At about three years of age, a mare can give birth. After it mates with a stallion, the mare gives birth in about one year. This usually happens in the springtime. The baby is called a foal.

It is best to pet and handle a foal each day beginning a few hours after it is born so it won't be afraid of people.

The foal relies on its mother's milk for food during its first three months.

Right after birth the mother licks its foal to clean and comfort it and to keep it warm. The foal rests for about 15 minutes. Then it tries standing on its awkward legs. Its legs are very wobbly. But as its legs become steady, the foal stands firmly on all four. The foal begins drinking its mother's warm milk.

When the foal stops
drinking its mother's
milk, it is called a
WEANLING.

Six months have gone by. The foal is bigger. It frisks
around the meadow and nibbles the fresh green grass.
It is time for the foal to be weaned. Now the foal is called
a weanling.

YEARLING

When the horse is about two to three years old, it can be trained for riding.

Now the weanling is older. Its body has grown to fit its long, strong legs. When it is one year old, it is called a yearling. It is old enough to be taught simple tasks and good manners. Eventually it may have its own babies.

Horses and their young should be cared for properly by their owners at all times. Often a stable or barn protects the horses from bad weather. Inside, the horses are kept in stalls. The stalls must be kept clean. Horses must be kept well fed and watered.

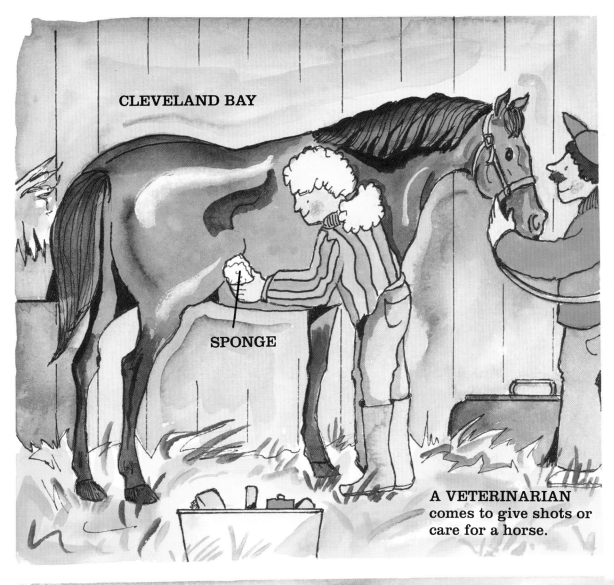

CLEVELAND BAY

SPONGE

A VETERINARIAN comes to give shots or care for a horse.

A HOOF PICK is used to clean the hoof.

PICK

HOOF OIL is used to keep the hooves from cracking or splitting.

A SOFT BRUSH is used to clean the short hair.

A hard-bristled DANDY BRUSH and a CURRYCOMB may be used to clean the long hair.

CURRYCOMB

DANDY BRUSH

Grooming means taking care of a horse's body. This should be done once daily. Grooming makes a horse look beautiful. An owner uses many different kinds of tools to groom a horse.

SOME WELL-KNOWN PUREBRED HORSES

THE ARABIAN is the oldest horse breed in the world.

The QUARTER HORSE gets its name from its speed at running the quarter-mile (.4 km) race.

The PALOMINO is often called the golden horse for its beautiful gold-colored coat.

The fastest animal in the world at running the mile is the THOROUGHBRED.

Different breeds of horses are known for their own special characteristics.

The spotted APPALOOSA (ap-a·LOO-sa) was first bred by the Nez Perce Indians.

MORGANS have worked at pulling plows and wagons and dragging logs. Today, most owners use them for riding.

The PERCHERON (PURR-shur-on) was the first breed of draft horses used in the United States. Today, it is often seen as a performing horse.

The CLYDESDALE is a handsome draft horse. Often teams of Clydesdales are seen pulling wagons in parades or shows.

They perform different tasks.

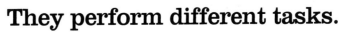

RODEO

QUARTER HORSE

CIRCUS

LIPIZZANER
(LIP-iz-on-er)

RACE

BLINDERS

THOROUGHBRED

HORSE SHOW

TENNESSEE WALKER

REINS

BRIDLE

SADDLE

BIT

STIRRUPS

All horse equipment is called TACK.

Horses appear in all kinds of events and contests. There are horse shows where prizes are given.

PALOMINO

Horses! Best of all they are good friends and companions.

CLIP ... CLOP ... CLIP ... CLOP ...

A domesticated horse usually lives to be between twenty and thirty years old. One horse lived to be more than sixty years old.

The largest breed of horse is the Shire. It stands 68 inches (170 cm) high at the withers. It can weigh more than 2,000 pounds (900 kg).

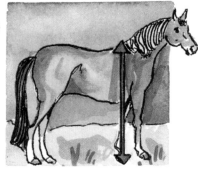

The average horse weighs about 1,000 pounds (450 kg) or more. It stands about 66 inches (165 cm) at the withers.

The life span of a wild horse usually is shorter because of the danger of living in the wild and the lack of medical care.

The smallest breed of horse is the Falabella. It stands about 30 inches (75 cm) high at the withers.

The Thoroughbred can run a mile (1.6 km) in about one-and-one-half minutes or at about 40 m.p.h. (64 km).

Stallions are bigger than mares of the same breed.

Many wonderful children's books have been written about horses. One story is titled *Black Beauty*.

Wild horses are protected by law.

The wild mustang descended from domestic horses that escaped. The name "mustang" comes from the Spanish word *mesteño*, meaning "strayed" or "wild."

An ends-up horseshoe is a symbol of good luck.

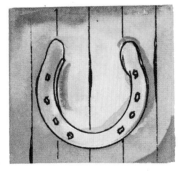